MEGADETH
Countdown to Extinction

Transcriptions by Hemme Luttjeboer, Danny Begelman,
Kenn Chipkin, and Alex Houton

ISBN 0-7935-3666-9

EMI MUSIC PUBLISHING

EXCLUSIVELY DISTRIBUTED BY

HAL•LEONARD
CORPORATION

7777 W. BLUEMOUND RD. P.O. BOX 13819 MILWAUKEE, WI 53213

DAVE MUSTAINE
LEAD & RHYTHM GUITAR
& LEAD VOCALS

MARTY FRIEDMAN
LEAD, RHYTHM & ACOUSTIC GUITAR
& BACKING VOCALS

NICK MENZA
DRUMS & BACKING VOCALS

DAVID ELLEFSON
BASS GUITAR
& BACKING VOCALS

SKIN O' MY TEETH
By
DAVE MUSTAINE

I had wrists donning slits
Flowing constantly
My broken body in a wreck
Wrapped around a tree
A crosswalk hit and run
The finish line for me
People clutter in the gutter
Take a look and see

Chorus
No escaping pain
You belong to me
Clinging on to life
By the skin o' my teeth

My blood flows through the streets
Deluge from the wounds
Empty jars of sleeping pills
On the dresser in my room
My wet brain neighbor cranes
His neck to see in time,
The white lights a train
Beating down on me

Chorus
Solo • Marty

I won't feel the hurt
I'm not trash any longer
That that doesn't kill me
Only makes me stronger
I need a ride to the morgue
That's what 911 is for
So, tag my toe and don't forget
Ooh to close the drawer

Chorus

© 1992 SCREEN GEMS-EMI MUSIC INC. and MUSTAINE MUSIC
All rights controlled and administered by SCREEN GEMS-EMI MUSIC
INC.
All Rights Reserved

SYMPHONY OF DESTRUCTION
By
DAVE MUSTAINE

You take a mortal man,
And put him in control
Watch him become a god,
Watch peoples heads a' roll
A 'roll…

Chorus
Just like to Pied Piper
Led rat through the streets
We dance like marionettes
Swaying to the Symphony…
Of Destruction

Acting like a robot
Its metal brain corrodes.
You try to take its pulse,
Before the head explodes,
Explodes…

Chorus
Solo • Marty

The earth starts to rumble
World powers fall
A 'warring for the heavens,
A peaceful man stands tall
Tall…

Chorus

© 1992 SCREEN GEMS-EMI MUSIC INC. and MUSTAINE MUSIC
All rights controlled and administered by SCREEN GEMS-EMI MUSIC
INC.
All Rights Reserved

ARCHITECTURE OF AGGRESSION
By
DAVE MUSTAINE and DAVE ELLEFSON

Born from the dark,
In the black cloak of night,
To envelop its prey below,
Deliver to the light,
To eliminate your enemy,
Hit them in their sleep,
And when all is won and lost,
The spoils of wars are yours to keep.

Chorus
Great nations built from the bones of the dead,
With mud and straw, blood and sweat,
You know your worth when your enemies
Praise your architecture of aggression.

Solo • Marty

Ensuing power vacuum,
A toppled leader dies
His body fuels the power fire,
And the flames rise to the sky.
One side of his face a kiss,
The other genocide.
Time to pay with your ass,
A worldwide suicide.

Chorus
Solo • Marty

Born from the dark,
In the black cloak of night,
To envelop its prey below,
Deliver to the light.
To eliminate your enemy,
Hit them in their sleep,
And when all is won and lost,
The spoils of wars are yours to keep.

Chorus

© 1992 SCREEN GEMS-EMI MUSIC INC., MUSTAINE MUSIC and
VULGARIAN MUSIC
All rights controlled and administered by SCREEN GEMS-EMI MUSIC
INC.
All Rights Reserved

FORECLOSURE OF A DREAM
By
DAVE MUSTAINE and DAVE ELLEFSON

Rise so high, yet so far to fall.
A plan of dignity and balance for all.
Political breakthrough, euphoria's high.
More borrowed money, more borrowed time.
Backed in a corner, caught up in the race.
Means to an end ended in disgrace.
Perspective is lost in the spirit of the chase.

Chorus
Foreclosure of a dream,
Those visions never seen,
Until all is lost,
Personal Holocaust,
Foreclosure of a dream.

Barren land that once filled a need,
Are worthless now, dead without a deed.
Slipping away from an iron grip,
Nature's scales are forced to tip,
The heartland cries, loss of all pride.
To leave ain't believing, so try and be tried.
Insufficient funds, insanity and suicide.

Chorus
Solo • Dave

Now with new hope some will be proud.
This is no hoax, no one pushed out.
Receive a reprieve and be a pioneer.
Break new ground of a new frontier.
New ideas will surely get by.
No deed, or dividend. Some may ask "Why?"
You'll find the solution, the answers in the sky.

Solo • Marty

Rise so high, yet so far to fall.
A plan of dignity and balance for all.
Political breakthrough, euphoria's high.
More borrowed money, more borrowed time.

Chorus'
Holocaust

© 1992 SCREEN GEMS-EMI MUSIC INC., MUSTAINE MUSIC and
VULGARIAN MUSIC
All rights controlled and administered by SCREEN GEMS-EMI MUSIC
INC.
All Rights Reserved

SWEATING BULLETS
By
DAVE MUSTAINE

Hello me… Meet the real me.
And my misfits way of life.
A dark black past is my
Most valued possession.
Hindsight is always 20-20.
But looking back it's still a bit fuzzy.
Speak of mutally assured destruction?
Nice story… Tell it to Reader's Digest!!!

Chorus
Felling paranoid
True enemy or false friend?
Anxiety's attacking me, and
My air is getting thin.
I'm in trouble for the things
I haven't got to yet.
I'm chomping at the bit, and my
Palms are getting wet, sweating bullets.

Solo • Dave

Hello me… It's me again.
You can subdue, but never tame me.
It gives me a migraine headache
Thinking down to your level,
Yea, just keep on thinking its my fault
And stay an inch or two outta kicking distance.
Mankind has got to know
His limitations

Chorus
Feeling claustrophobic,
Like the walls are closing in.
Blood stains on my hands and
I don't know where I've been.
I'm in trouble for the things
I haven't got to yet.
I'm sharpening the axe and my
Palms are getting wet, sweating bullets.

Well, me… it's nice talking to myself.
A credit to dementia.
Some day you too will know my pain,
And smile its blacktooth grin.
If the war inside my head
Won't take a day off I'll be dead.
My icy fingers claw your back,
Here I come again.

Chorus
Feeling paranoid
True enemy or false friend?
Anxiety's attacking me
And my air is getting thin
Feeling claustrophobic
Like the walls are closing in
Blood stains on my hands
And I don't know where I've been
Once you committed me
Now you've acquitted me
Claiming validity
For your stupidity
I'm chomping at the bit
I'm sharpening the axe
Here I come again, whoa!
Sweating bullets

THIS WAS MY LIFE
By
DAVE MUSTAINE

It was just another day
It was just another fight
It was words strung into sentences
It was doomed to not be right

There is something wrong with me
There is something wrong with you
There is nothing left of us
There is one thing I can do

Chorus
Lying on your bed,
Examining my head
This is the part of me that hates
Paybacks are a bitch
I throw the switch
Somewhere an electric chair awaits
Hey! This was my life
Hey! This was my fate

This was the wrong thing to do
This was the wrong one to be doing
This was the road to destiny
This was the road to my ruin

Now there's nothing for the suspect
Now there's nothing left to say
Now there's method to the madness
Now there's society to pay

Chorus
In our life there's if
In our beliefs there's lie
In our business there's sin
In our bodies there's die

Solo • Dave

This was my life
This was my fate

COUNTDOWN TO EXTINCTION
By
DAVE MUSTAINE, DAVE ELLEFSON,
NICK MENZA and MARTY FRIEDMAN

Endangered species, caged in fright,
Shot is cold blood, no chance to fight,
The stage is set, now pay the price,
An ego boost, don't think twice.
Technology, the battle's unfair,
You pull the hammer without a care.
Squeeze the trigger that makes you Man.
Pseudo-safari, the hunt is canned…
The hunt is canned.

Chorus
All is gone, all but one.
No contest, nowhere to run.
No more left, only one.
This is it, this is the Countdown to Extinction.

Tell the truth, you wouldn't dare.
The skin and trophy, oh so rare.
Silence speaks louder than words.
Ignore the guilt, and take your turn.
Liars anagram is "liars,"
Man you were never even there.
Killed a few feet from the cages,
Point blank, your so courageous…
So courageous.

Chorus

One hour from now,
another species of life form
will disappear off the face of the planet
forever… and the rate is accelerating

Chorus

HIGH SPEED DIRT
By
DAVE MUSTAINE and DAVE ELLEFSON

Do it if you dare
Leaping from the sky
Hurling thru the air
Exhilarating high
See the earth below
Soon to make a crater
Blue sky, black death
I'm off to meet my maker

Chorus
Energy of the gods, adrenalin surge
Won't stop till I hit the ground, I'm on my way for sure
Up here in the air, this will never hurt
I'm on my way to impact, taste the high speed dirt

Paralyzed with fear
Feel velocity gain
Entering a near
Catatonic state
Pressure of the sound
Roaring thru my head
Crash into the ground
Damned if I'll be dead

Chorus

Jump or die!

Solo • Dave
Solo • Marty

Dropping all my weight
Going down full throttle
The pale horse awaits
Like a genie in a bottle
Fire in my veins
Faster as I go
I forgot my name
I'm a dirt torpedo

Solo• Marty

High speed dirt…

Solo • Dave

PSYCHOTRON
By
DAVE MUSTAINE

Assassin in stealth
Assailant from Hell
Impervious to damage
Computer on board
Engaged in a war
Non-stop combatant
Maybe not a mutant, maybe a man

Chorus
Part bionic
and organic
Not a cyborg
Call him Psychotron

Burning inside
Godspeed in glide
Battle plan running
A killing machine
Just downright mean
And forever gunning
Maybe not a mutant, maybe a man

Chorus

Target to destroy
Arms in employ
Full assault fire threat
Sensors indicate
You will terminate
Life systems disconnect

Chorus

All Solos • Marty

Psychotron

CAPTIVE HONOUR
By
DAVE MUSTAINE, DAVE ELLEFSON
NICK MENZA and MARTY FREIDMAN

Madness comes, and madness goes
An insane place, with insane moves
Battles without, for battles within
Where evil lives and evil rules
Breaking them up, just breaking them in
Quickest way out, quickest relief wins
Never disclose. never betray
Cease to speak or cease to breathe
And when you kill a man, you're a murderer
Kill many, and you're a conqueror
Kill then all… Ooh… Oh you're a god!

Ladies and gentlemen of the jury,
Have you reached a verdict?

Yes, we have Your Honour, we find the defendant guilty!
On all counts for crimes against all humanity.

By virtue of the jury's decision and the power
Vested in my by the state I hereby sentence you to be
Incarcerated with no possibility of parole for life.

Life?… Whadda ya mean life?… I ain't got a life.

Boy?… Your soul better belong to Jesus!
Hmmm-mmm cause your ass belongs to me!

Chorus
Captive honour, ain't no honour

No time for questions
No time for the games
Start kicking ass
And taking down the names
A long shit list
A shorter fuse
He is untouchable
And guarantees you'll lose

Chorus
Solo • Dave

Inside the bighouse
His nightmare unfolds
Before he got there
His manpussy was sold
Black blanket welcome
This tough guy's now a bitch
Praying for death
It can't be worse than this

Chorus
Solo • Dave
Solo • Marty

Chorus

ASHES IN YOUR MOUTH
By
DAVE MUSTAINE, DAVE ELLEFSON,
NICK MENZA and MARTY FRIEDMAN

People have round shoulders from fairing heavy loads.
And the soldiers liberate them, laying mines along their roads.
Sorrow paid for valor is too much to recall
Of the countless corpses piled up along the wailing wall.

Melting down all metals, turning plows and shears to swords,
Shun words of the Bible, we need implements of war.
Chalklines and red puddles of those who have been slain
Destiny, that crooked schemer, says the dead shall rise again.

Chorus
Where do we go from here?
And should we really care?
The end is finally here.
God have mercy!

Now we've rewritten history,
The one thing we've found out,
Sweet taste of vindication,
It turns to ashes in your mouth.

Chorus

If you're fighting to live
It's O.K. to die!
The answer to your question is…
Welcome to tomorrow!

Solo • Marty • Marty • Dave

Where do we go from here?
God have mercy!

Chorus

Countdown to Extinction

CONTENTS

NOTATION LEGEND

SKIN O' MY TEETH

By
DAVE MUSTAINE

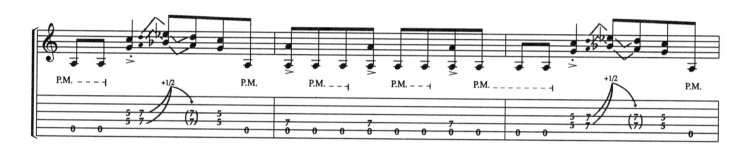

*2 Guitars arranged for 1

10

D.S. ℅ al Coda ⊕

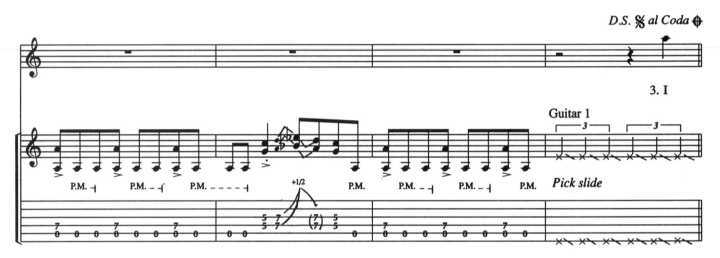

3. I

Pick slide

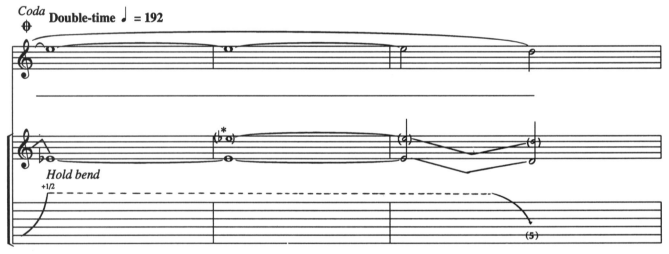

*Octave feedback

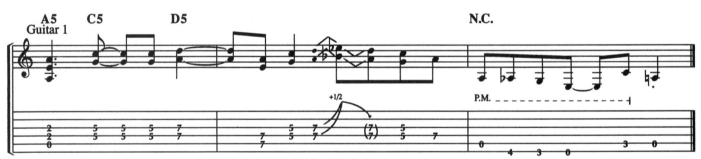

Additional Lyrics

Verse 2: My blood flows through the streets
Deluge from the wounds
Empty jars of sleeping pills
On the dresser in my room
My wet brain neighbor cranes
His neck to see in time
The white lights a train
Bearing down on me

Verse 3: I won't feel the hurt
I'm not trash any longer
That that doesn't kill me
Only makes me stronger
I need a ride to the morgue
That's what 911 is for
So tag my toe and don't forget
Ooh to close the drawer

SYMPHONY OF DESTRUCTION

By
DAVE MUSTAINE

1. You take a mor-tal man,
2.3. *See additional lyrics*

an' put him in con-trol.

*2 Guitars arranged as one.

Rhythm Fill 1
Guitars 1 & 2

*Upper note overdub.
**Overdub.

Sym-pho-ny. Just like the Pied_____ Pip - er led_____ rats through_____ the streets. We dance like the

Guitar 3

P.M.

Guitars 1 & 2

Let ring throughout

Fill 1
Guitar 4

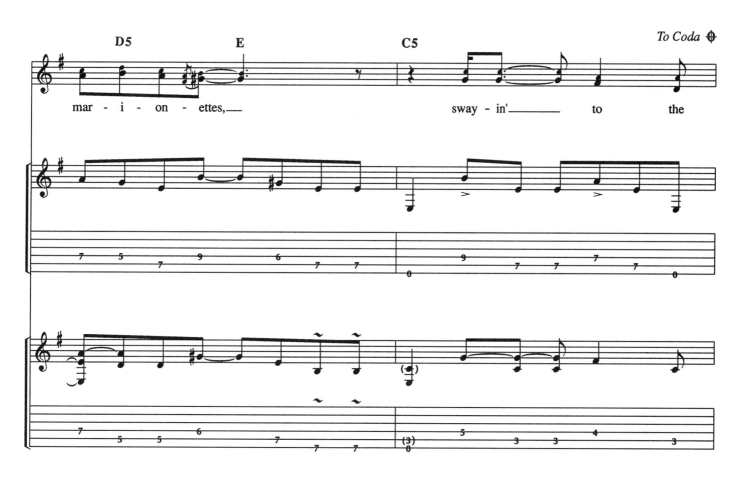

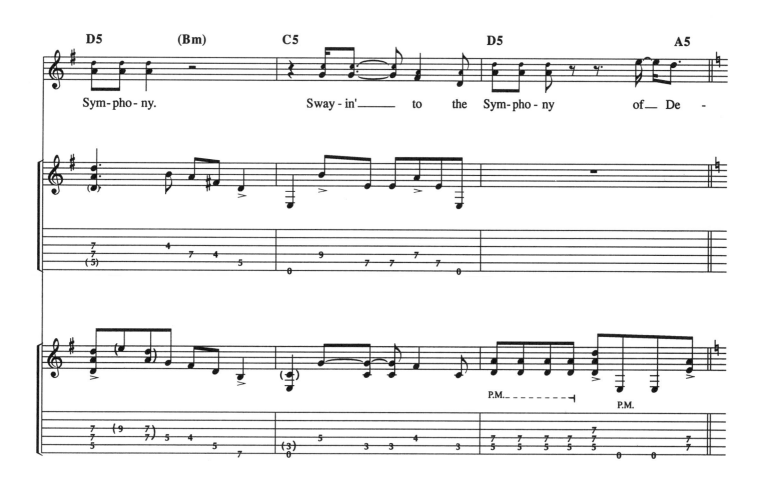

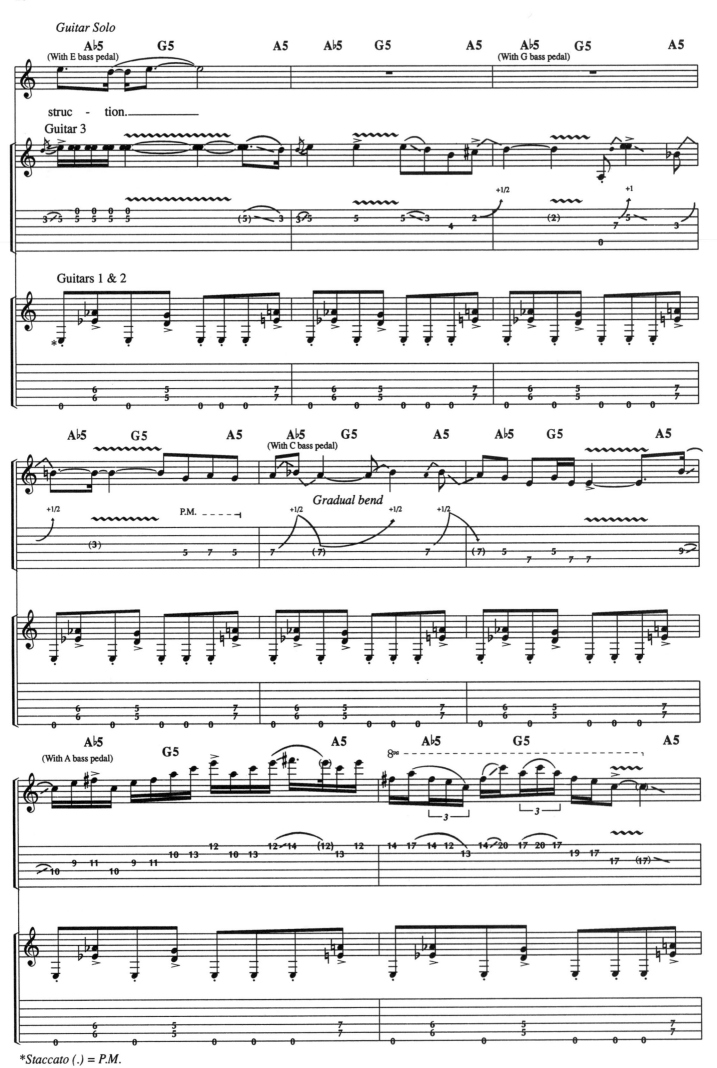

*Staccato (.) = P.M.

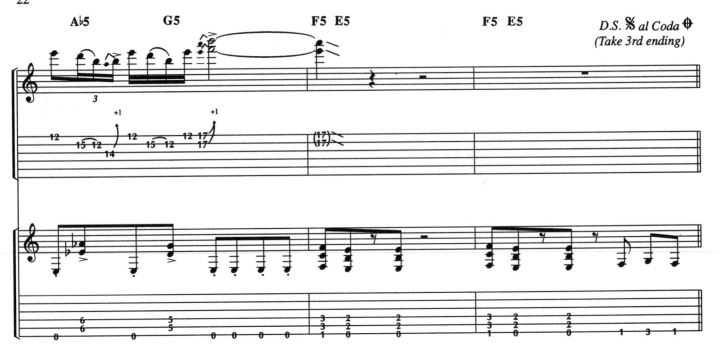

Additional Lyrics

Verse 2:   Acting like a robot
It's metal brain corrodes
Try to take it's pulse
Before the head explodes, explodes, explodes, ah. . .

Verse 3:   The earth starts to rumble
World powers fall
Warring for the heavens
A peaceful man stands tall, tall, tall. . .

ARCHITECTURE OF AGGRESSION

By
DAVE MUSTAINE and DAVE ELLEFSON

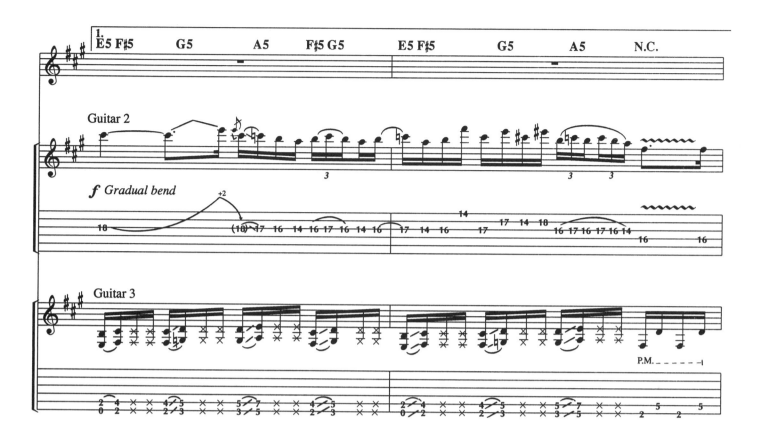

Praise your ar - chi - tec-ture of ag - gres - sion, — ah.

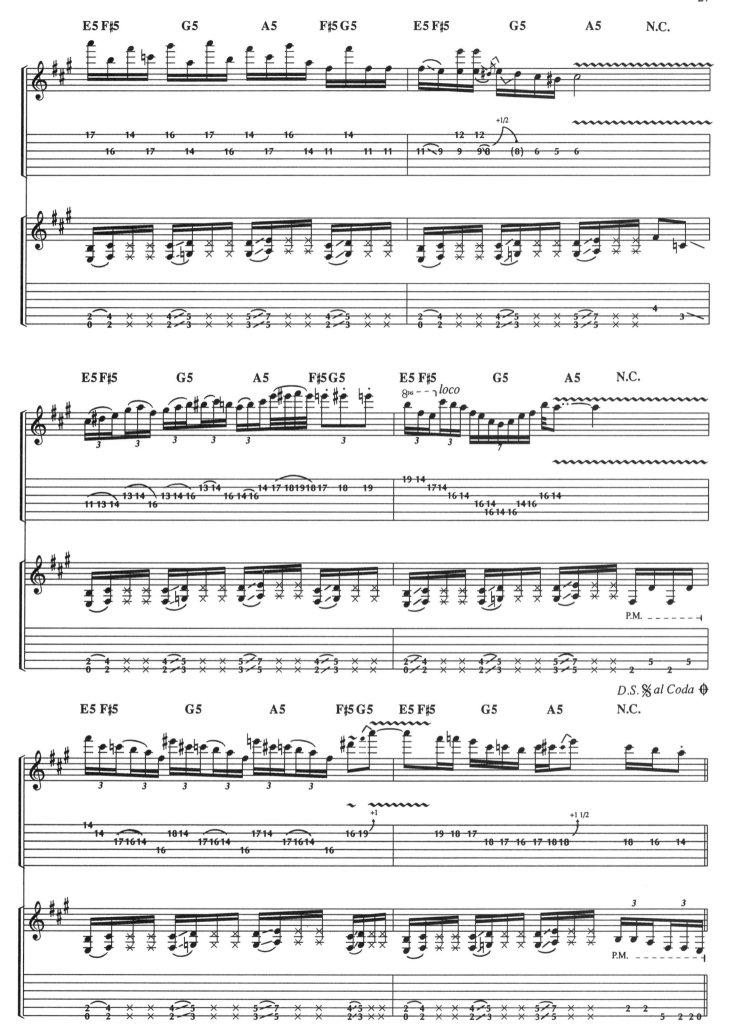

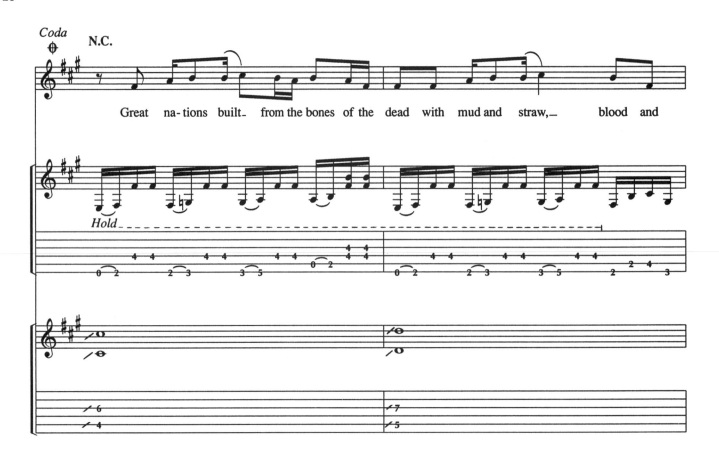

Great na-tions built_ from the bones of the dead with mud and straw,_ blood and

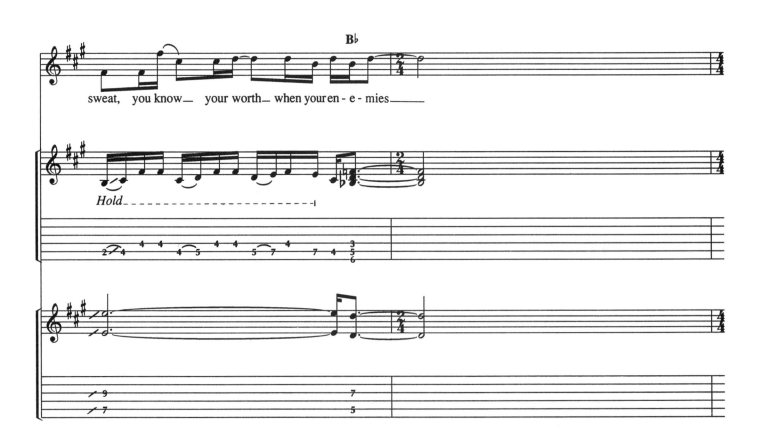

sweat, you know_ your worth_ when your en - e - mies_

N.C. **E5 F♯5**

praise your__ ar - chi - tec - ture of ag - gres sion._____

Additional Lyrics

Verse 2: Ensuing power vacuum as a toppled leader dies
His body fuels the power fire, and the flames rise to the sky.
One side of his face a kiss, the other genocide.
Time to pay with your ass, a worldwide suicide.

Great nations are built from the bones of the dead.
With mud and straw, and blood and sweat.
You know your worth when your enemies
Praise your architecture of aggression.

Praise your architecture of aggression.

Verse 3: Born from the dark, in the black cloak of night.
To envelope it's prey below to deliver to the light.
To eliminate your enemy, you hit them in their sleep,
And when all is won and lost, the spoils of war are yours to keep.

Great nations are built from the bones of the dead.
With mud and straw, and blood and sweat.
You know your worth when your enemies
Praise your architecture of aggression.

Great nations are built from the bones of the dead.
With mud and straw, and blood and sweat.

FORECLOSURE OF A DREAM

By
DAVE MUSTAINE and **DAVE ELLEFSON**

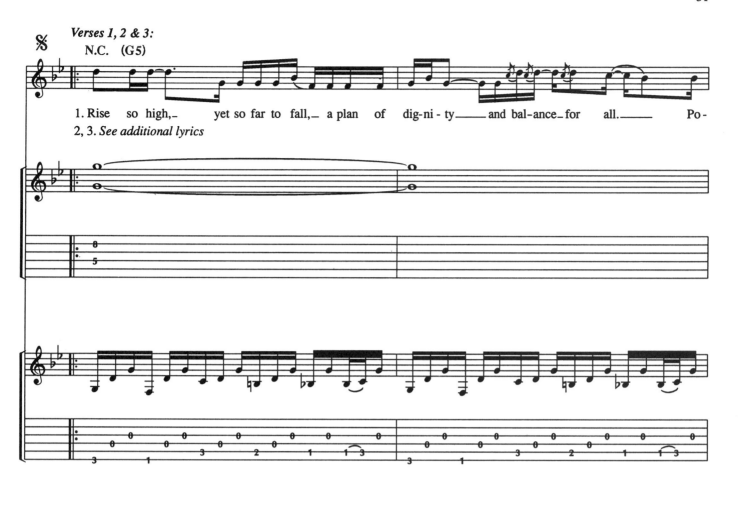

Verses 1, 2 & 3:
N.C. (G5)

1. Rise so high,— yet so far to fall,— a plan of dig-ni-ty———— and bal-ance—for all.——— Po-
2, 3. *See additional lyrics*

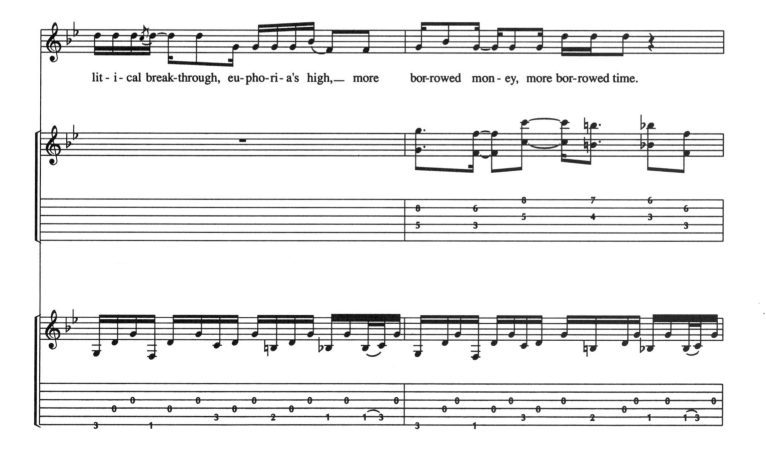

lit - i - cal break-through, eu-pho-ri-a's high,— more bor-rowed mon - ey, more bor-rowed time.

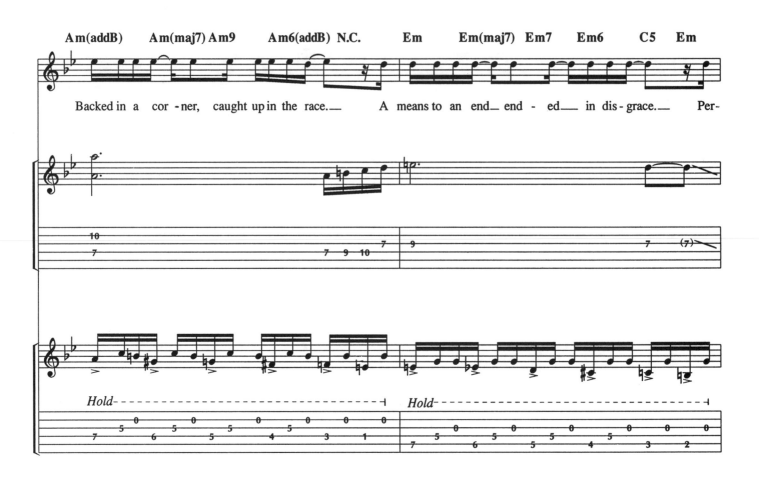

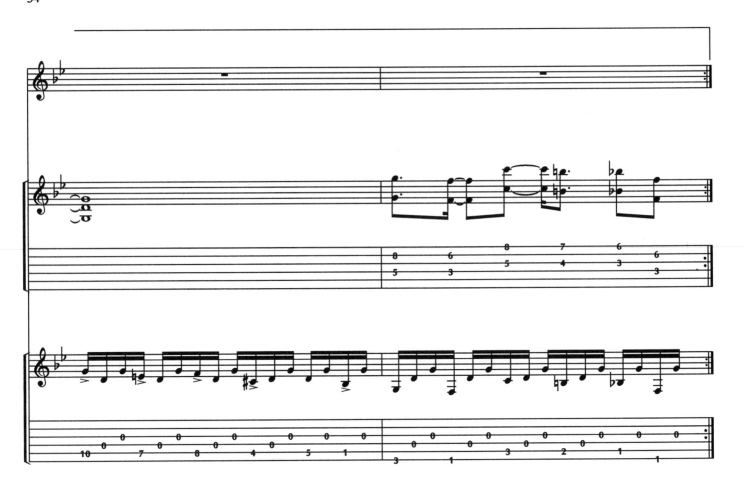

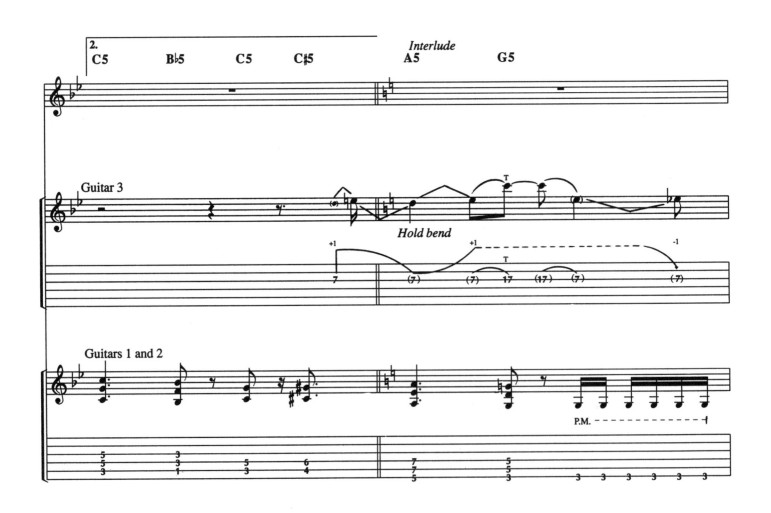

*Vocal tacet

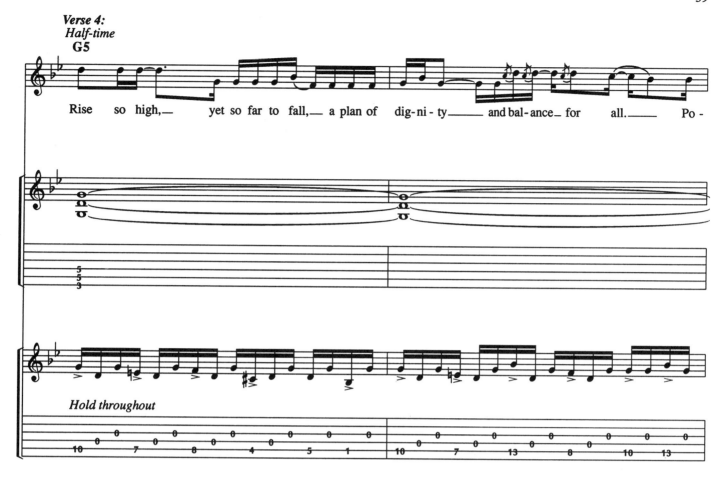

Additional Lyrics

Verse 2: Barren land that once filled a need,
Are worthless now, dead without a deed.
Slipping away from an iron grip,
Natures scales are forced to tip.
The heartland cries, loss of all pride
To leave ain't believing, so try and be tried,
Insufficient funds, insanity and suicide.

Verse 3: Now with new hope some will be proud,
This is no hoax, no one pushed out,
Receive a reprieve and be a pioneer,
Break new ground of a new frontier,
New ideas will surely get by,
No deed, or dividend,
Some will ask "Why?"
You'll find the solution, the answer's in the sky.

SWEATING BULLETS

By
DAVE MUSTAINE

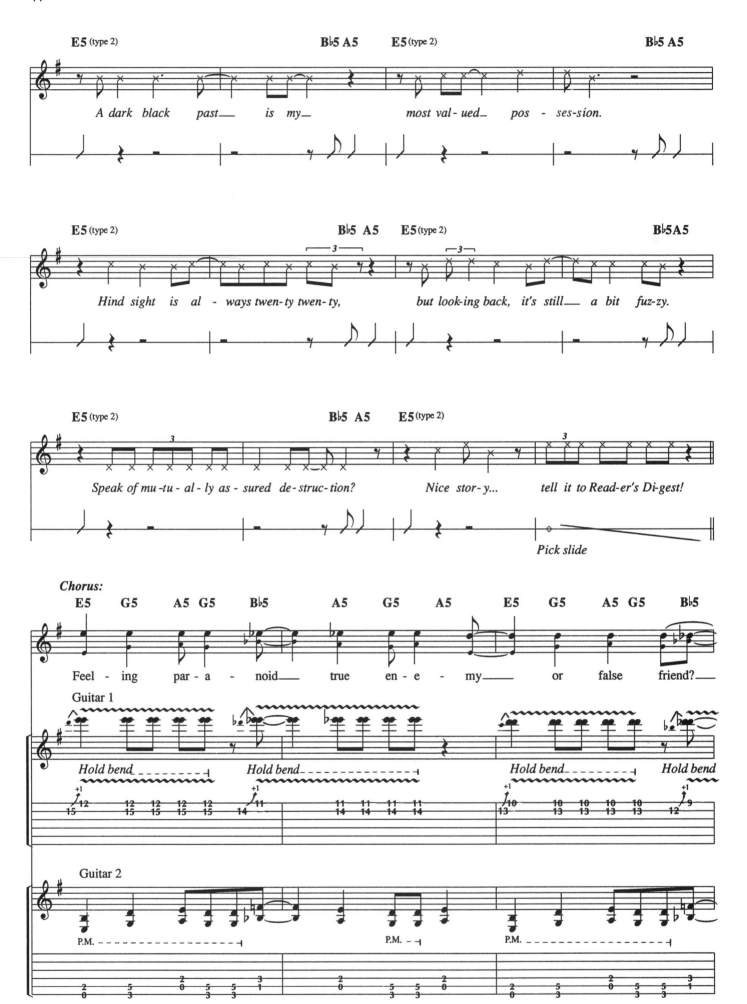

46

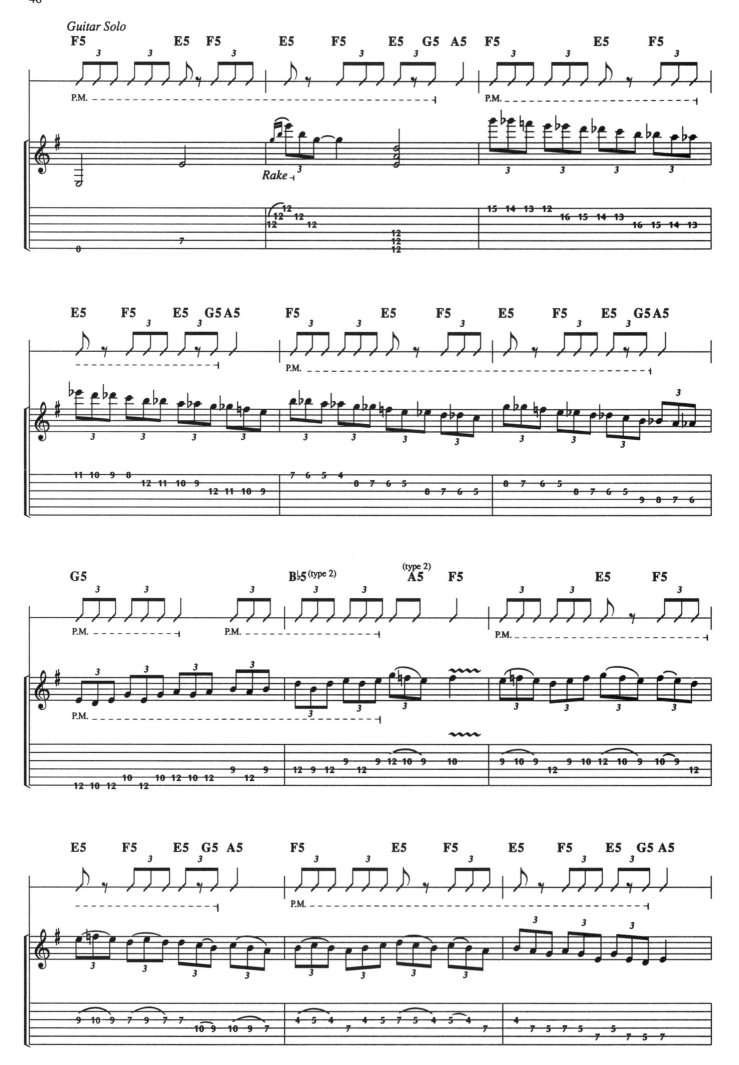

Double time triplet feel

E5

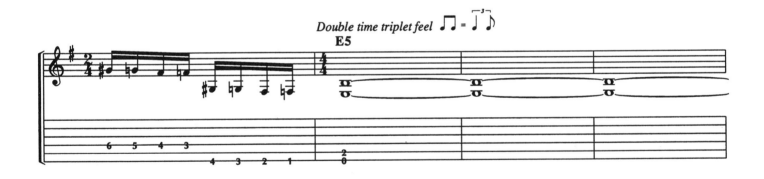

D.S. % al Coda

B♭5   A5

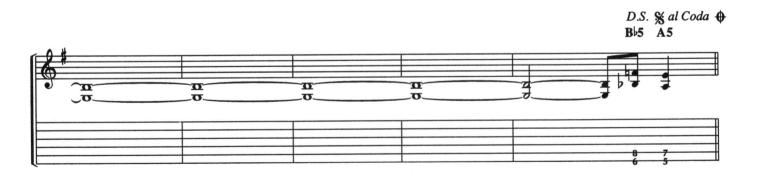

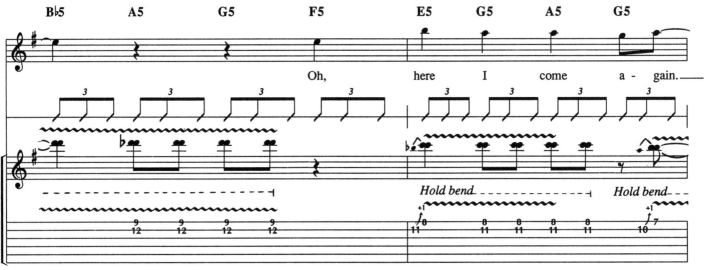

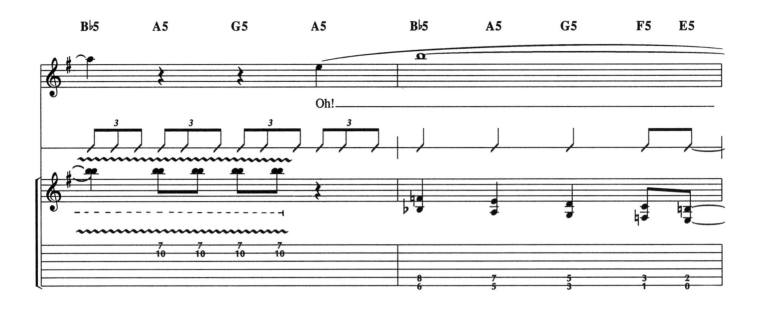

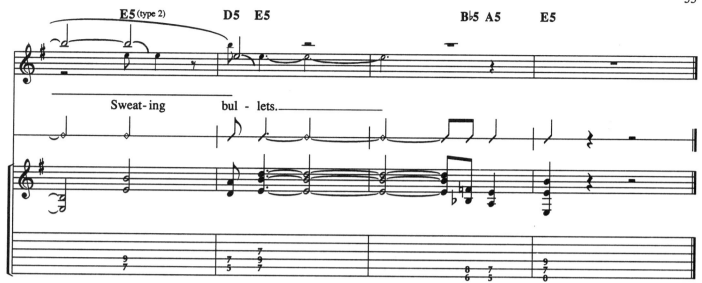

Additional Lyrics

Verse 2: Hello me... It's me again.
You can subdue, but never tame me.
It gives me a migraine headache
Thinking down to your level
Yea, just keep on thinking it's my fault
And stay an inch or two outta kicking distance
Mankind has got to know
His limitations.

Chorus 2: Feeling claustrophobic
Like the walls are closing in
Bloodstains on my hands and
I don't know where I've been.
I'm in trouble for the things
I haven't got to yet
I'm sharpening the axe and my
Palms are getting wet, sweating bullets.

Verse 3: Well, me... it's nice talking to myself
A credit to dementia.
Some day you too will know my pain
And smile it's blacktooth grin
If the war inside my head
Won't take a day off I'll be dead
My icy fingers claw your back,
Here I come again.

THIS WAS MY LIFE

By
DAVE MUSTAINE

* 2 Guitars arranged as 1

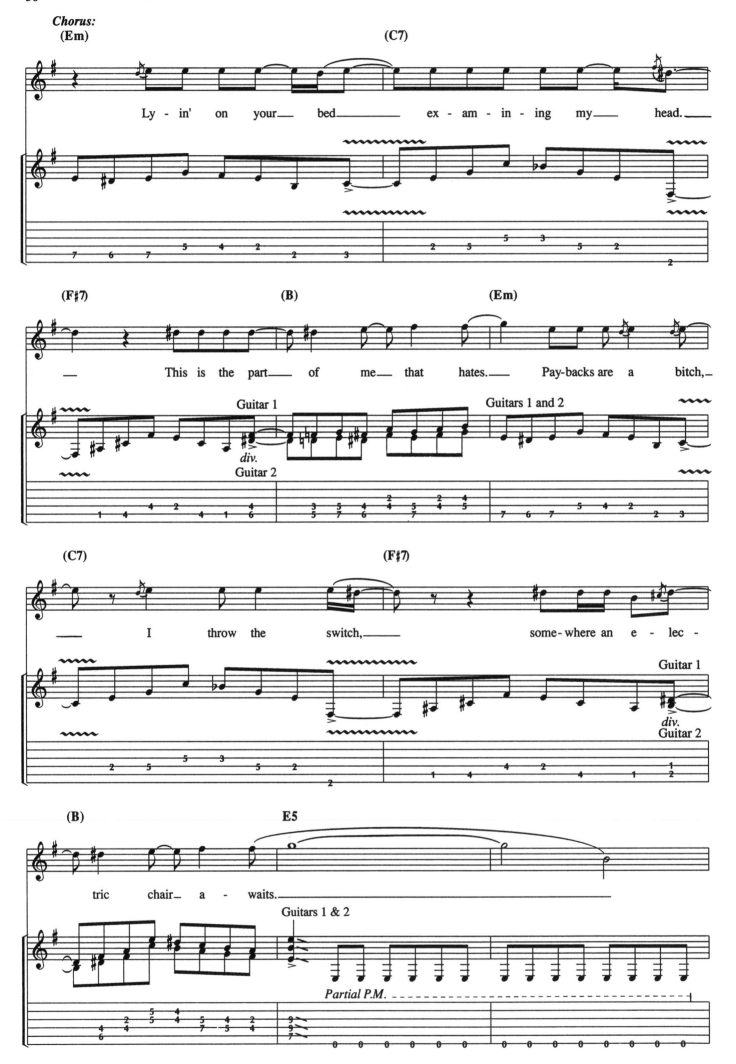

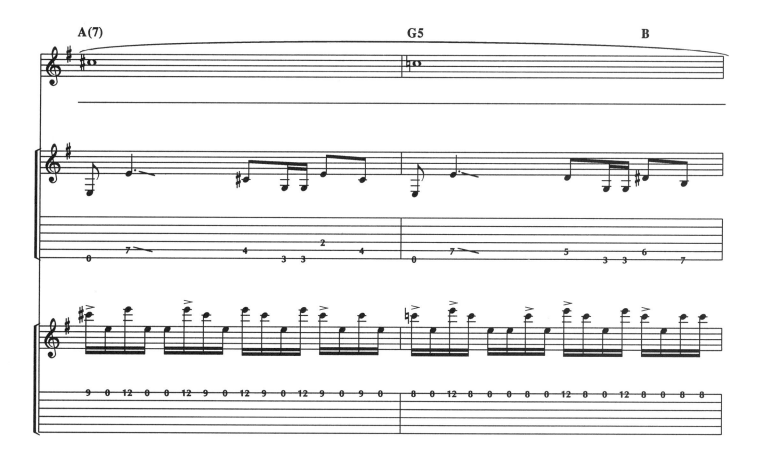

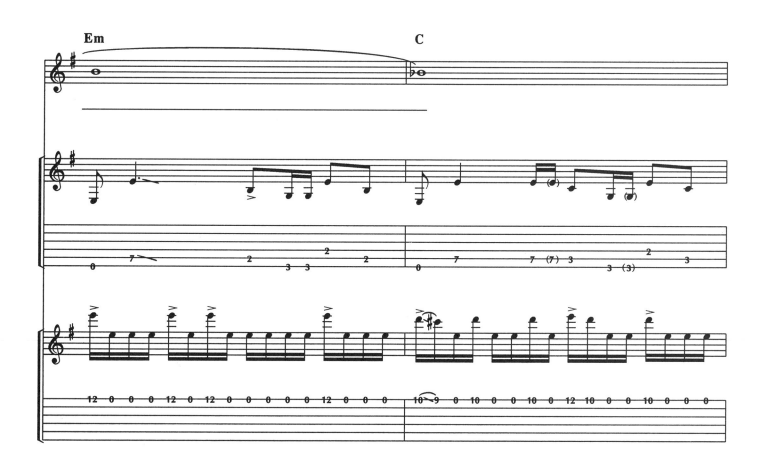

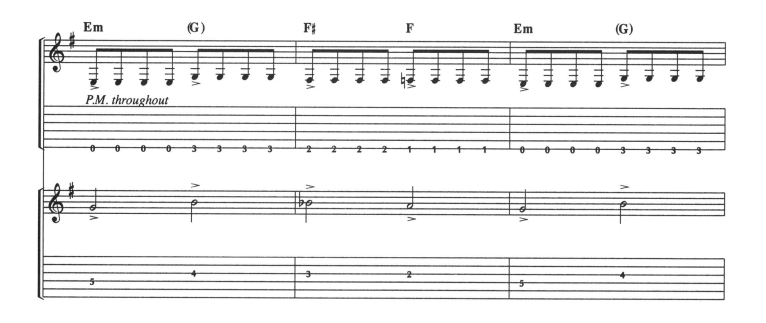

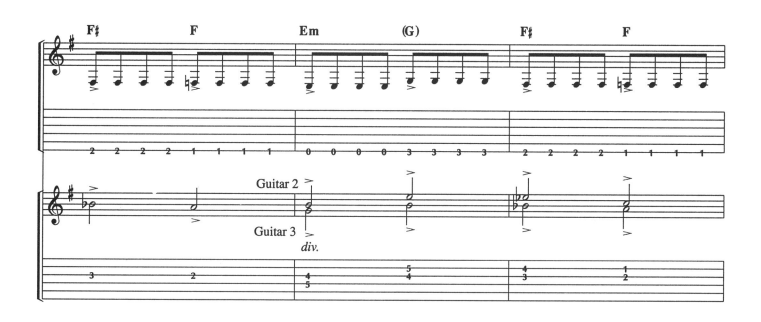

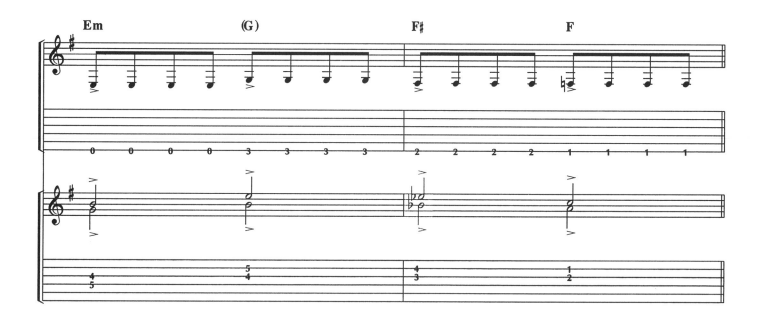

Outro:

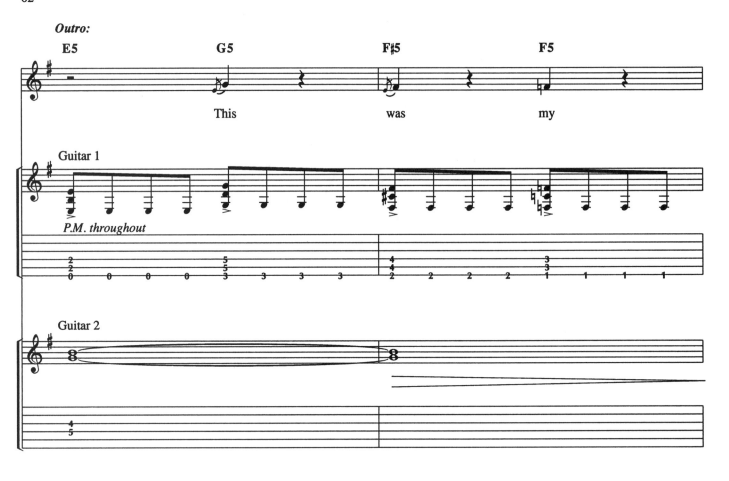

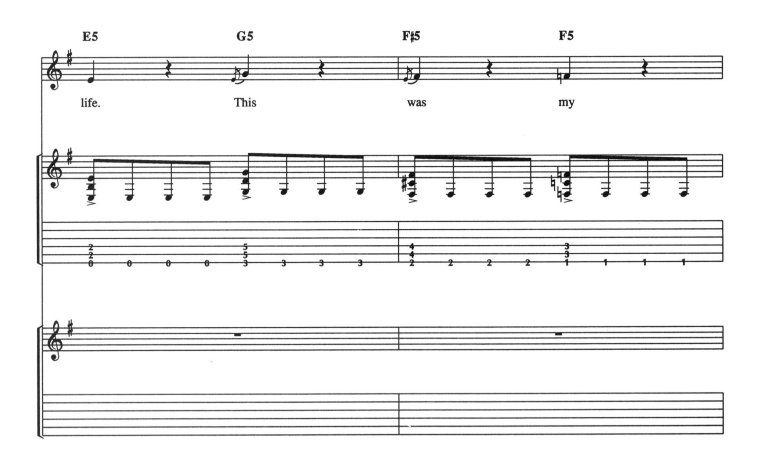

COUNTDOWN TO EXTINCTION

By
DAVE MUSTAINE, DAVE ELLEFSON,
NICK MENZA and MARTY FRIEDMAN

Verse 1:

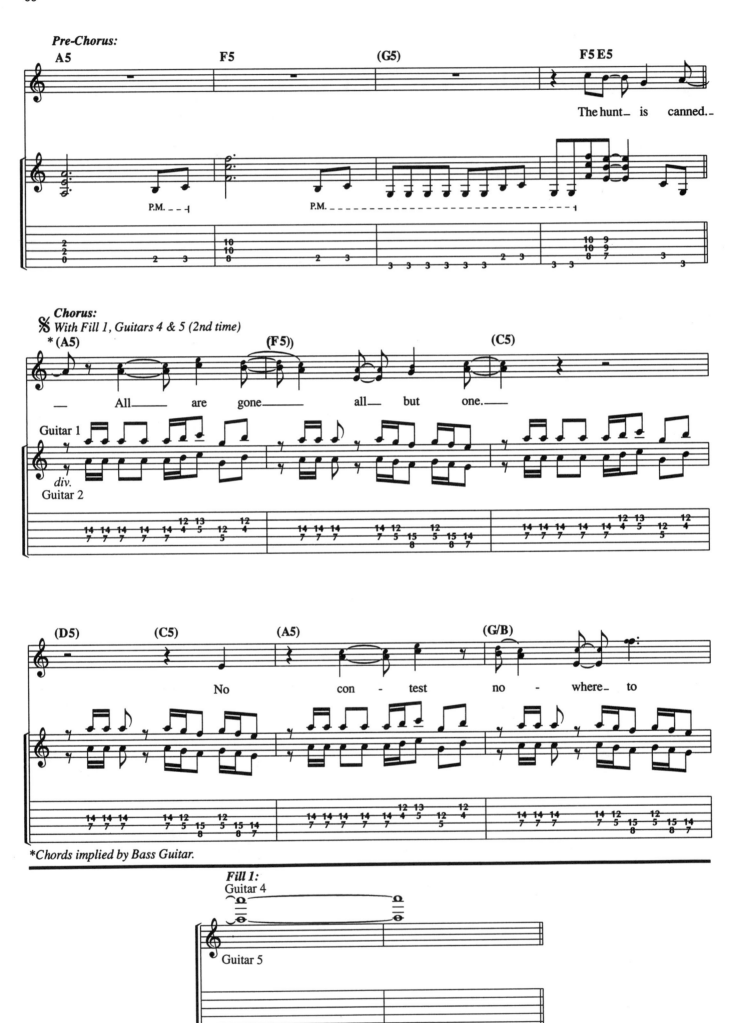

The hunt is canned.

All are gone all but one.

No con-test no-where to

*Chords implied by Bass Guitar.

Verse 2:

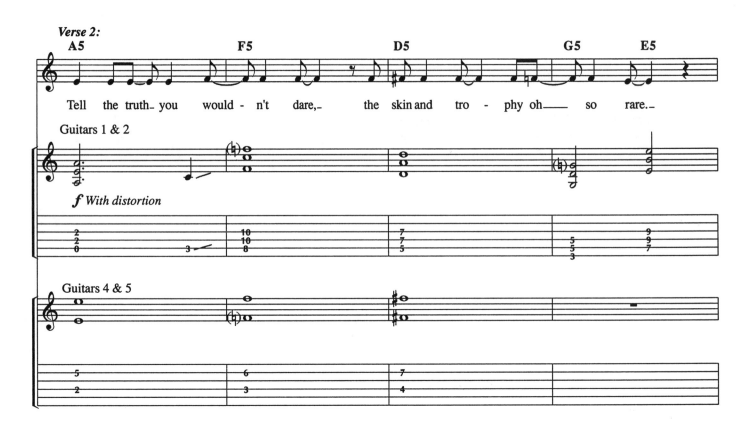

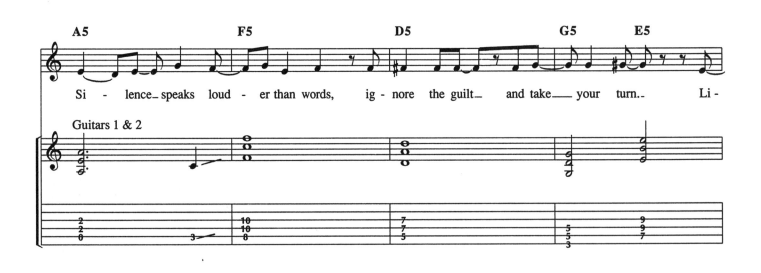

Chords implied by Bass Guitar.

Chords implied by Bass Guitar.

*Chords are implied from Guitar voicings.
**2 Guitars arranged for 1

HIGH SPEED DIRT

By
DAVE MUSTAINE and DAVE ELLEFSON

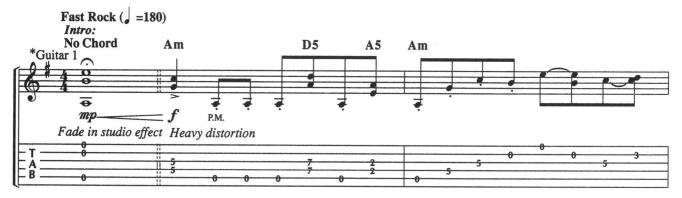

Staccato notes (.) = palm mute

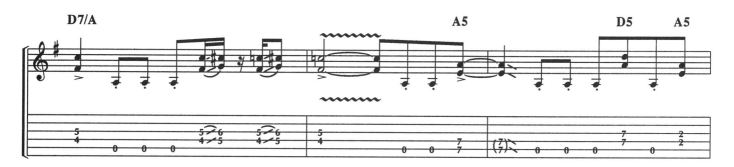

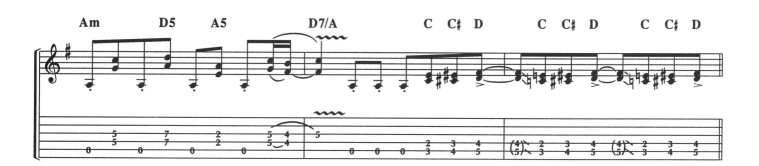

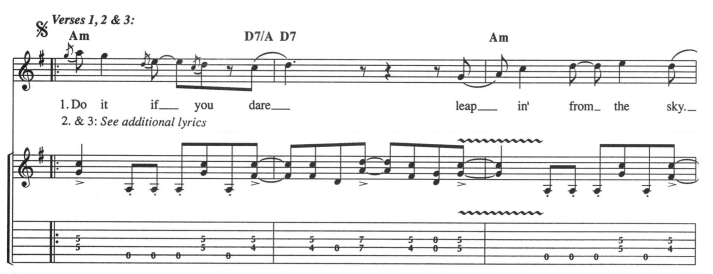

1. Do it if__ you dare__ leap__ in' from__ the sky.__
2. & 3: See additional lyrics

*2 Guitars arranged as one.

*On D.S.

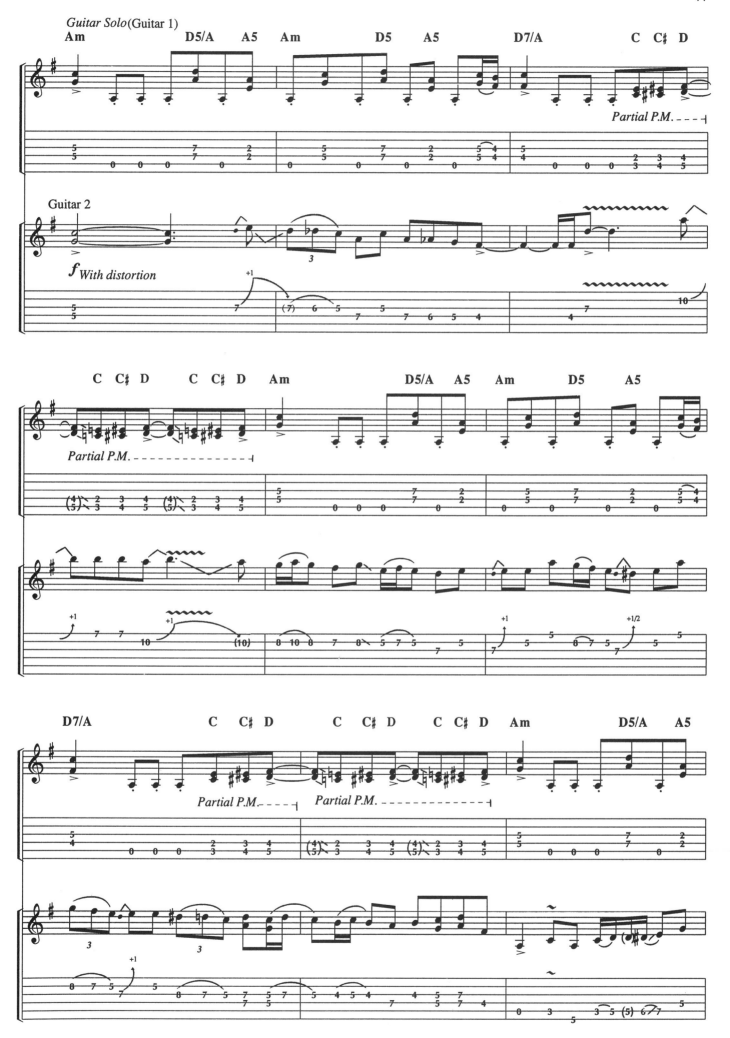

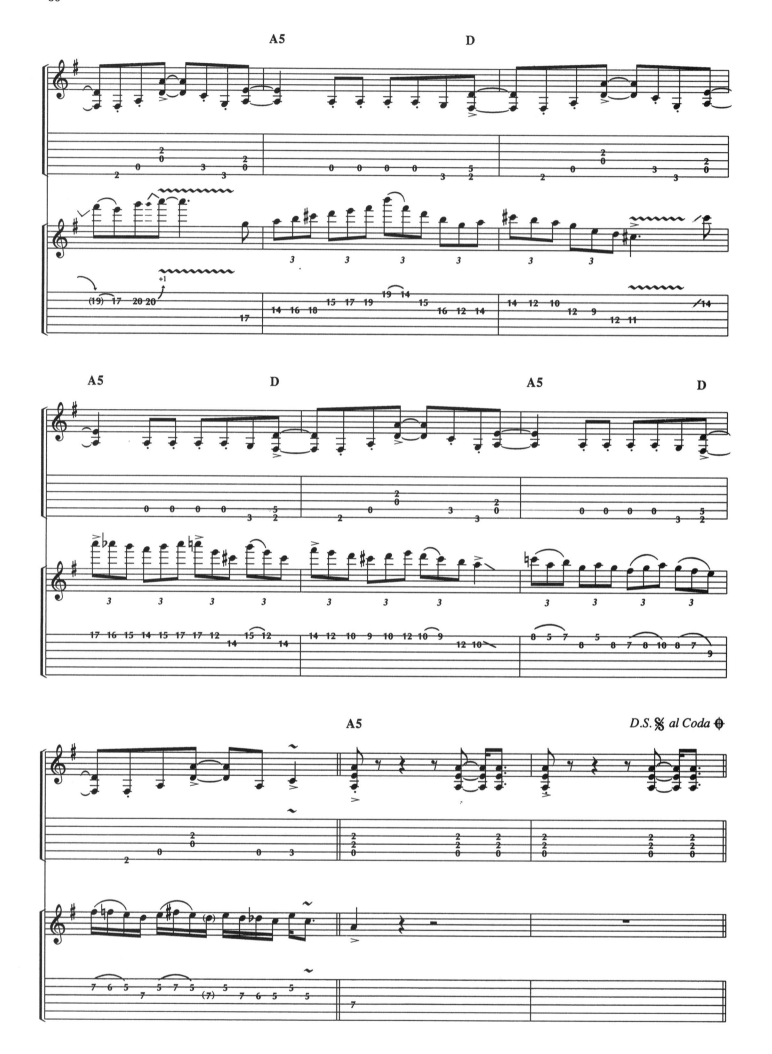

82

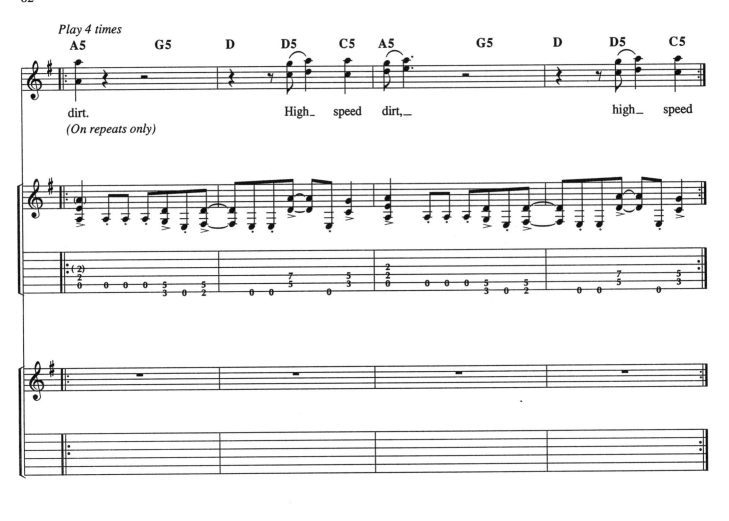

Outro:

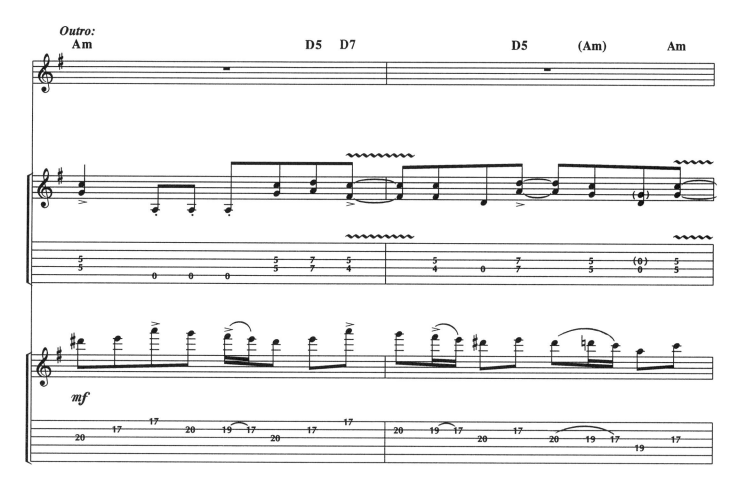

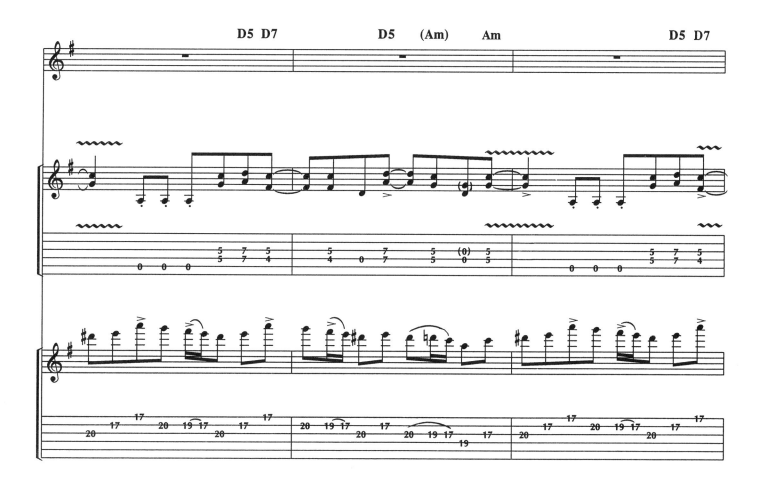

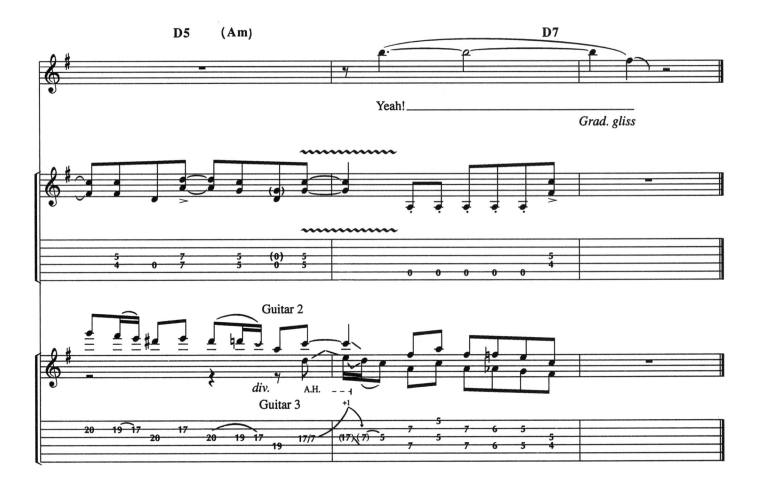

Additional Lyrics

Verse 2:   Paralyzed with fear
Feel velocity gain
Entering a near
Catatonic state
Pressure of the sound
Roaring thru my head
Crashing to the ground
Damned if I'll be dead

Verse 3:   Dropping all my weight
Going down full throttle
The pale horse awaits
Like a genie in a bottle
Fire in my veins
Faster as I go
I forgot my name
I'm a dirt torpedo

PSYCHOTRON

By
DAVE MUSTAINE

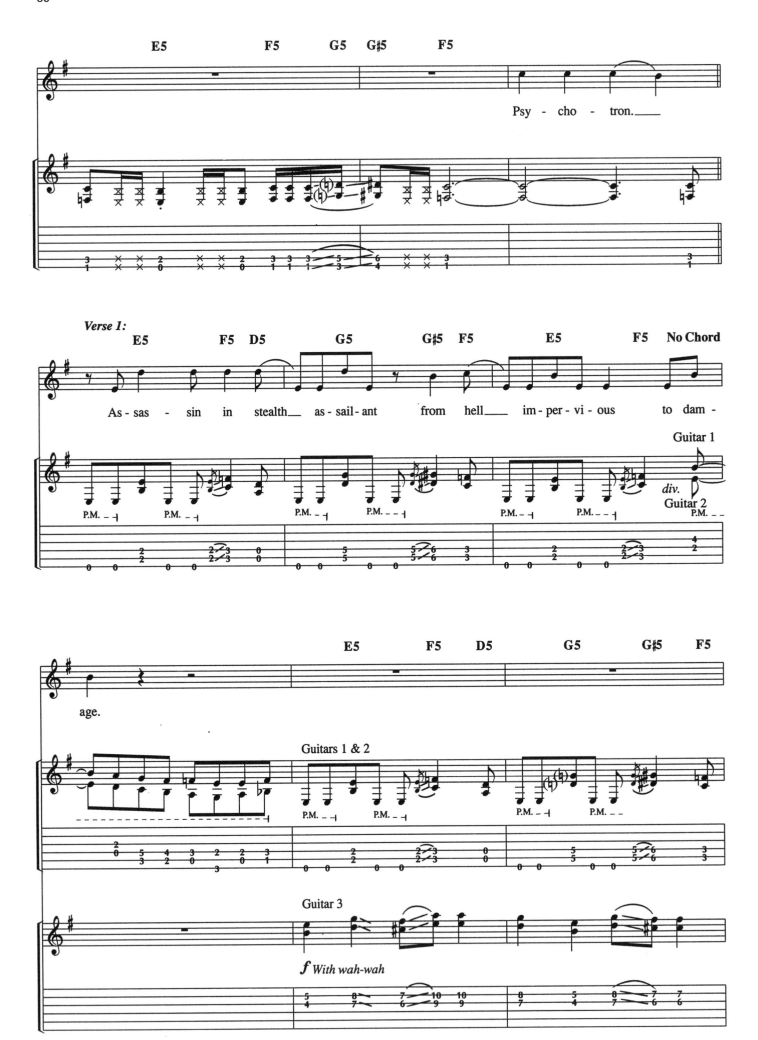

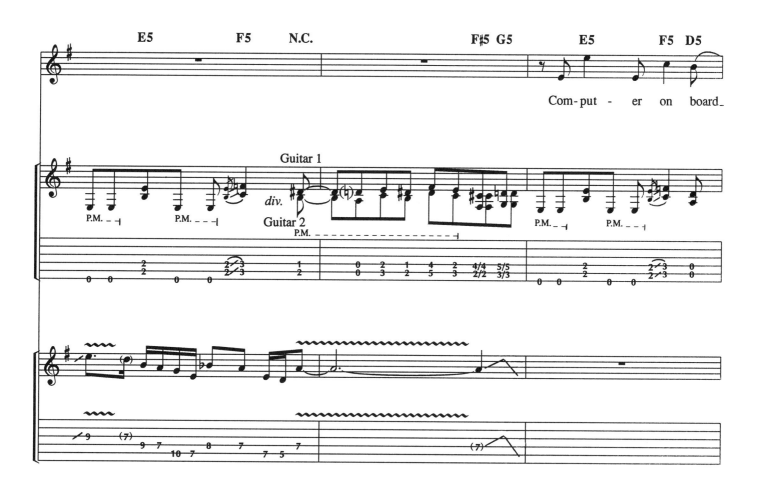

Com-put - er on board

_ en - gaged in a war,_ non - stop com-bat - ant.

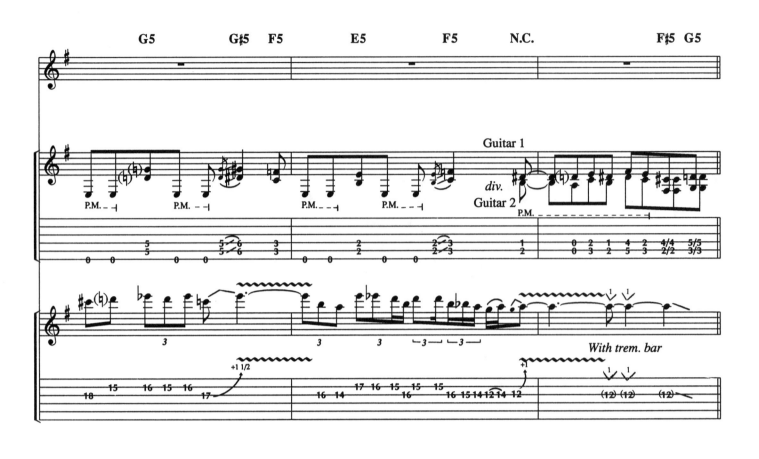

Pre-Chorus:

May - be not, not a mu - tant, may - be_ a man.____

Chorus:

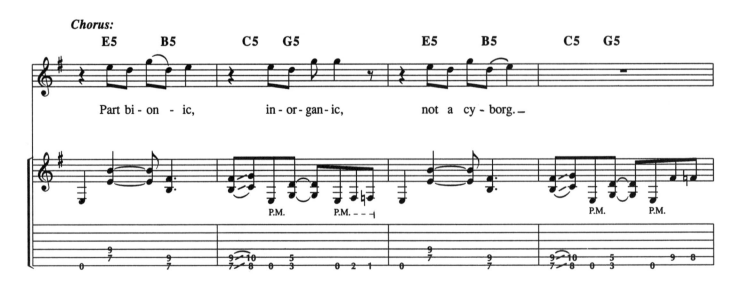

Part bi - on - ic, in - or - gan - ic, not a cy - borg._

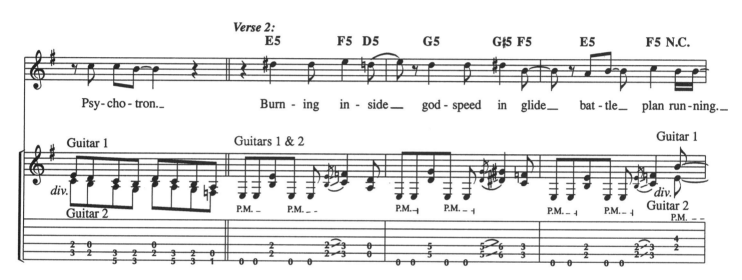

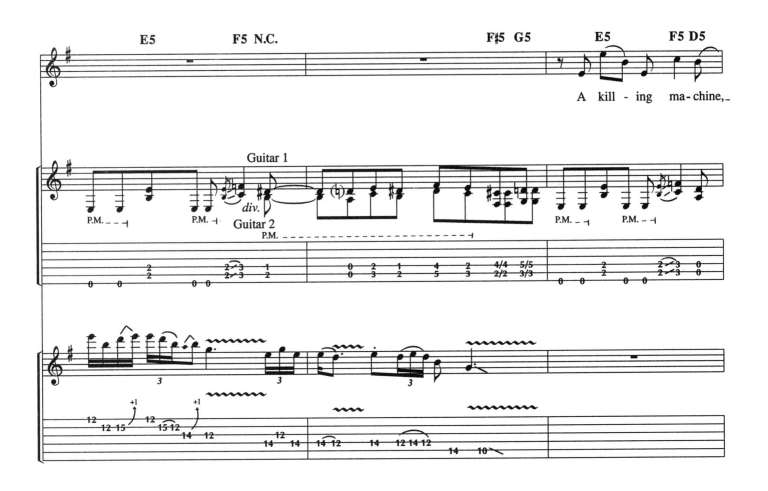

Part bi - on - ic, in - or - gan - ic,

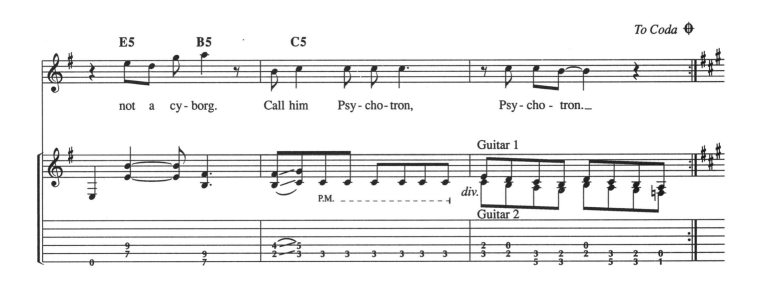

not a cy - borg. Call him Psy - cho - tron, Psy - cho - tron.

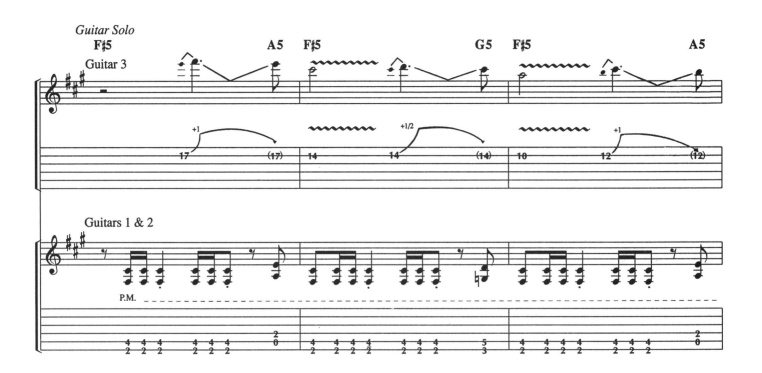

Verse 3:

Tar - get to de - stroy_____ arms in em - ploy_____ full as - sault fire__

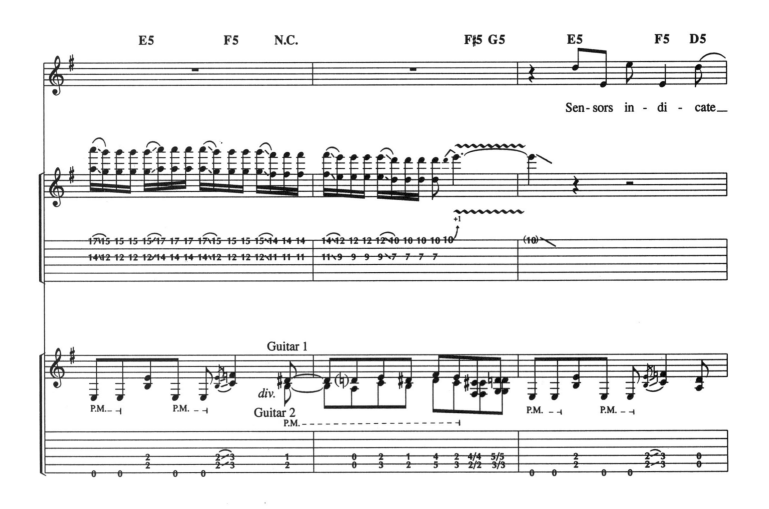

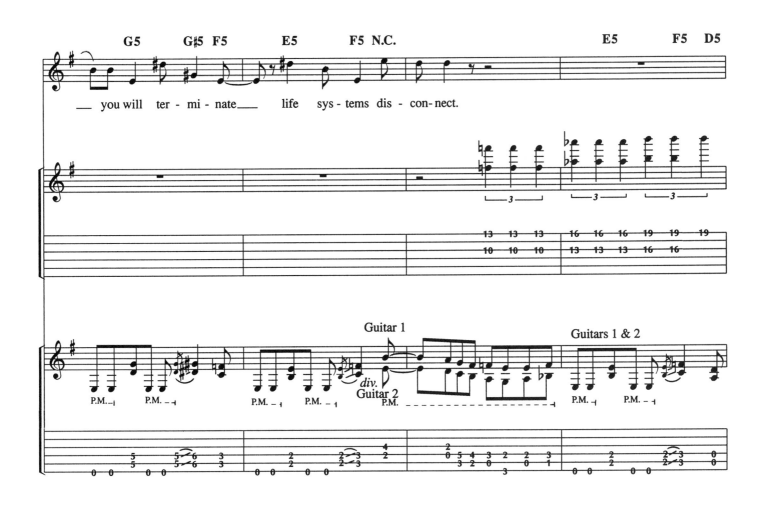

you will ter - mi - nate life sys - tems dis - con - nect.

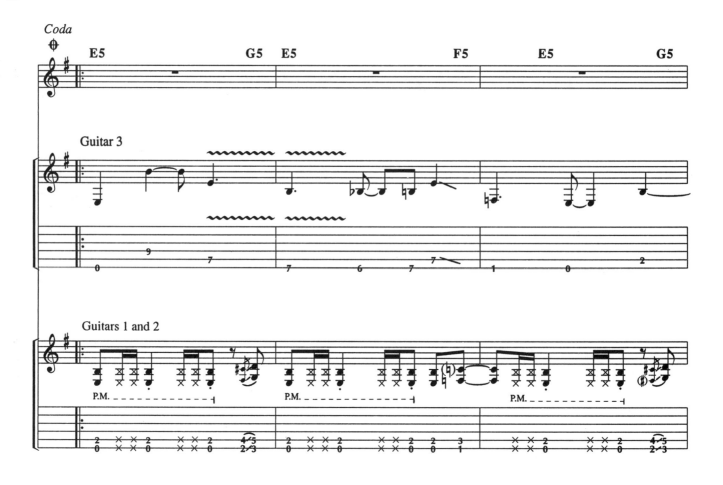

CAPTIVE HONOUR

By
DAVE MUSTAINE, DAVE ELLEFSON,
NICK MENZA and MARTY FRIEDMAN

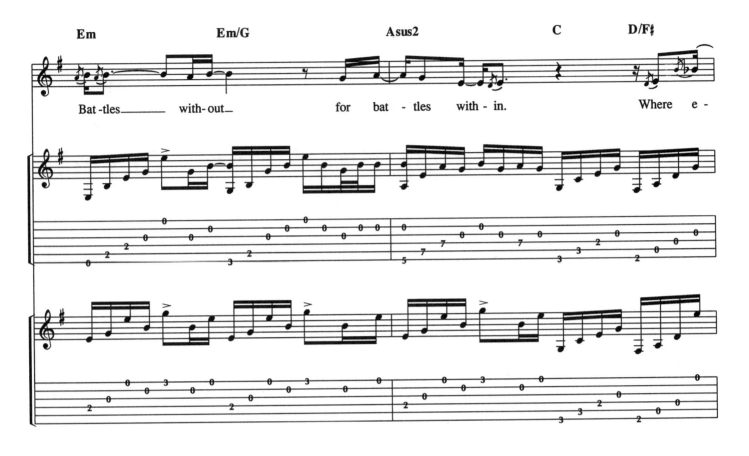

Bat -tles_____ with-out____ for bat - tles with - in. Where e -

vil lives____ an' e - vil___ rules._____

Break-in' them up, just break-in' them in.— Quick-est way out, quick-est re - lief

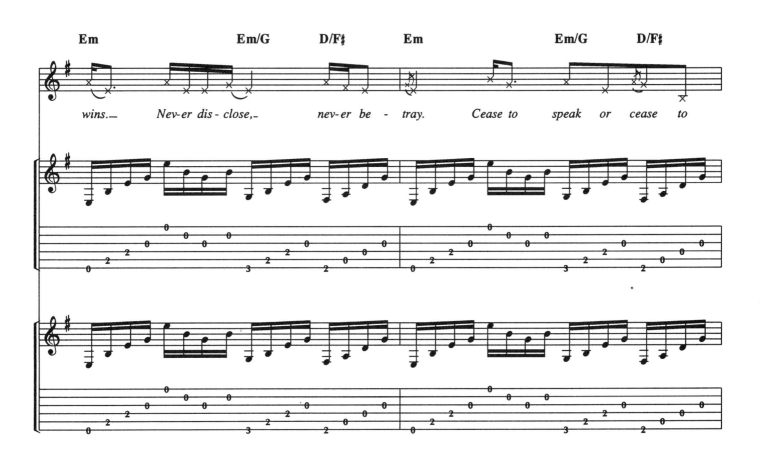

wins.— Nev-er dis - close,— nev-er be - tray. Cease to speak or cease to

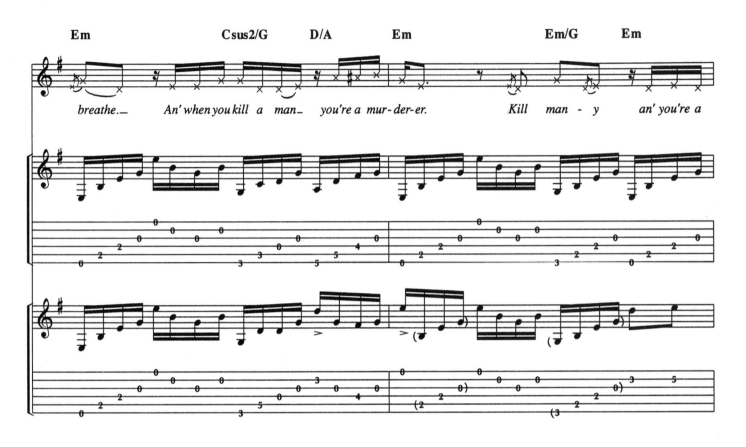

* *On repeat only. End of Solo 1, Guitar 4*

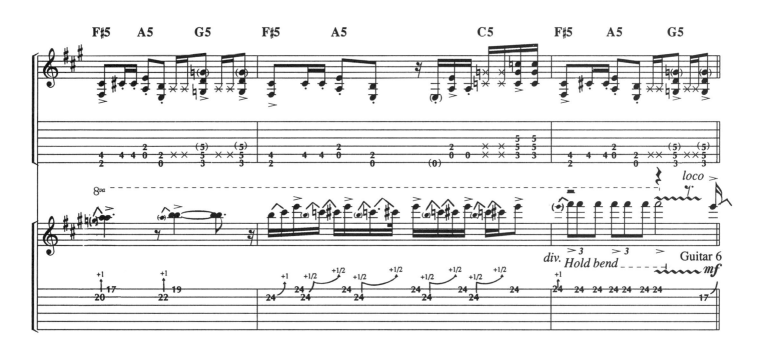

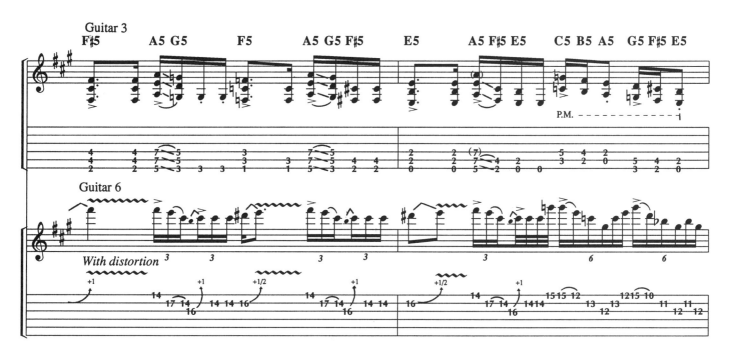

Cap - tive hon - our,__ ain't no hon - our.____

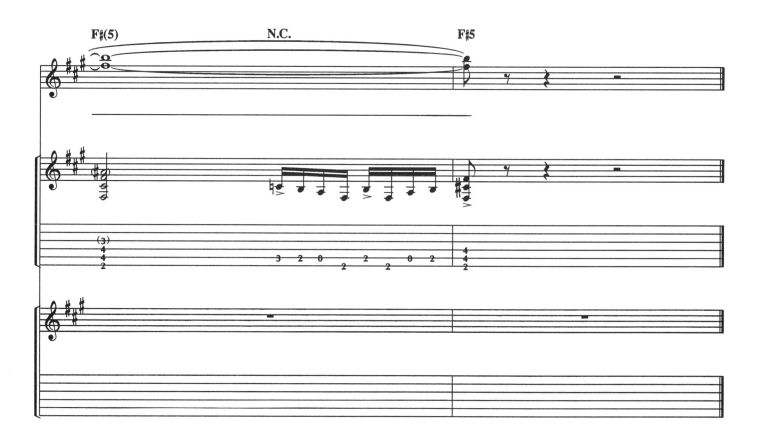

ASHES IN YOUR MOUTH

By
DAVE MUSTAINE, DAVE ELLEFSON,
NICK MENZA and MARTY FRIEDMAN

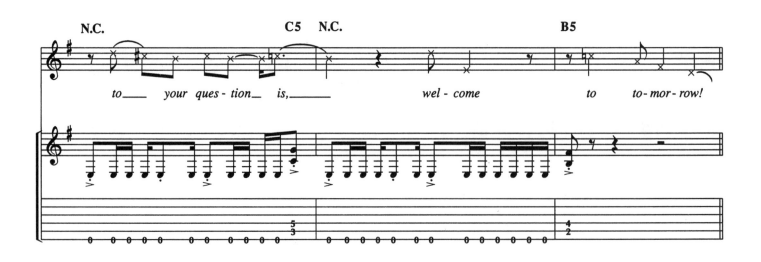

to___ your ques - tion___ is,___ wel - come to to - mor - row!

Guitar Solo 1

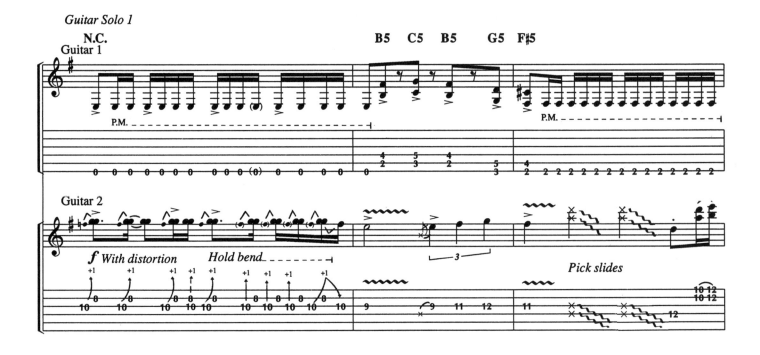

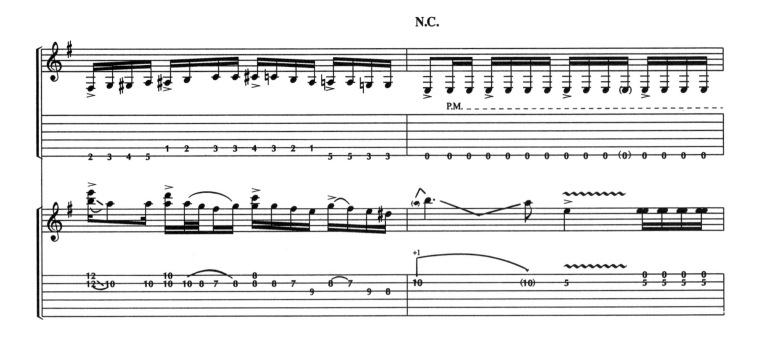

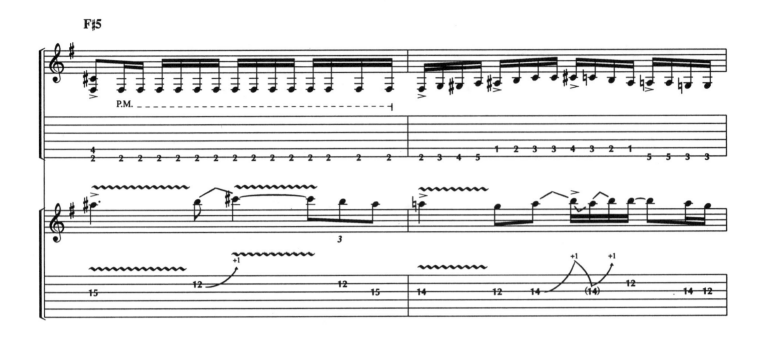

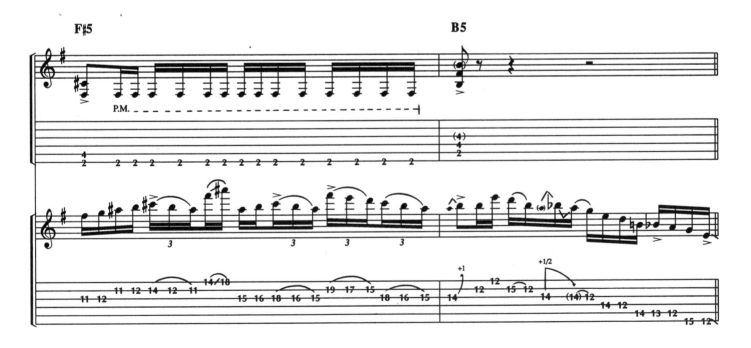

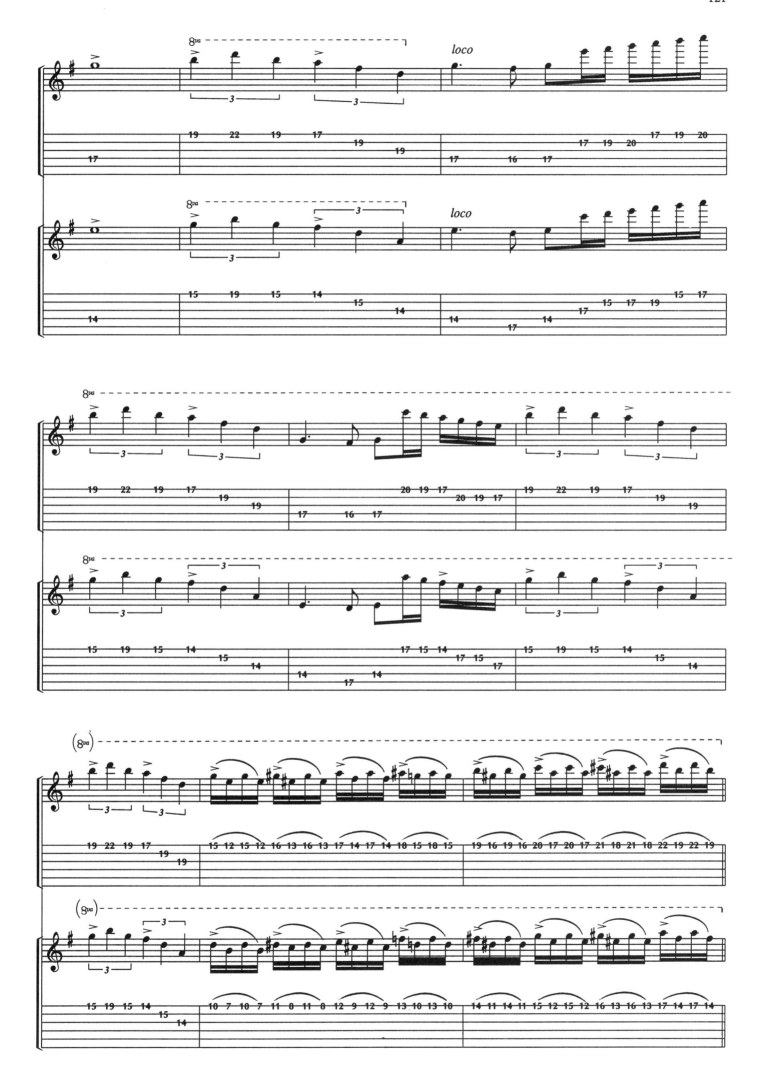

*With feedback pitch = B

RECORDED VERSIONS
GUITAR
RECORDED VERSIONS
The Best Note-For-Note Transcriptions Available

ALL BOOKS INCLUDE TABLATURE

00694909 Aerosmith – Get A Grip	$19.95
00692015 Aerosmith's Greatest Hits	$18.95
00660133 Aerosmith – Pump	$18.95
00694865 Alice In Chains – Dirt	$18.95
00660225 Alice In Chains – Facelift	$18.95
00694826 Anthrax – Attack Of The Killer B's	$18.95
00660227 Anthrax – Persistence Of Time	$18.95
00694797 Armored Saint – Symbol Of Salvation	$18.95
00694876 Chet Atkins – Contemporary Styles	$18.95
00660051 Badlands	$18.95
00694880 Beatles – Abbey Road	$18.95
00694832 Beatles For Acoustic Guitar	$18.95
00660140 Beatles Guitar Book	$18.95
00694891 Beatles – Revolver	$18.95
00694863 Beatles – Sgt. Pepper's Lonely Hearts Club Band	$18.95
00694884 The Best of George Benson	$19.95
00692385 Chuck Berry	$18.95
00692200 Black Sabbath – We Sold Our Soul For Rock 'N' Roll	$18.95
00694821 Blue Heaven – Great Blues Guitar	$18.95
00694770 Jon Bon Jovi – Blaze Of Glory	$18.95
00694871 Bon Jovi – Keep The Faith	$18.95
00694774 Bon Jovi – New Jersey	$18.95
00694775 Bon Jovi – Slippery When Wet	$18.95
00694762 Cinderella – Heartbreak Station	$18.95
00692376 Cinderella – Long Cold Winter	$18.95
00692375 Cinderella – Night Songs	$18.95
00694875 Eric Clapton – Boxed Set	$75.00
00692392 Eric Clapton – Crossroads Vol. 1	$22.95
00692393 Eric Clapton – Crossroads Vol. 2	$22.95
00692394 Eric Clapton – Crossroads Vol. 3	$22.95
00660139 Eric Clapton – Journeyman	$18.95
00694869 Eric Clapton – Unplugged	$18.95
00692391 The Best of Eric Clapton	$18.95
00694896 John Mayall/Eric Clapton – Bluesbreakers	$18.95
00694873 Eric Clapton – Timepieces	$18.95
00694788 Classic Rock	$17.95
00694793 Classic Rock Instrumentals	$16.95
00694837 Albert Collins – The Complete Imperial Records	$18.95
00694862 Contemporary Country Guitar	$18.95
00660127 Alice Cooper – Trash	$18.95
00694840 Cream – Disraeli Gears	$14.95
00694844 Def Leppard – Adrenalize	$18.95
00692440 Def Leppard – High 'N' Dry/Pyromania	$18.95
00692430 Def Leppard – Hysteria	$18.95
00660186 Alex De Grassi Guitar Collection	$16.95
00694831 Derek And The Dominos – Layla & Other Assorted Love Songs	$19.95
00692240 Bo Diddley Guitar Solos	$18.95
00660175 Dio – Lock Up The Wolves	$18.95
00660178 Willie Dixon	$24.95
00694915 Electric Blues Guitar Giants	$18.95
00694852 Electric Blues Volume 1 – Book/Cassette Pack	$22.95
00694800 FireHouse	$18.95
00694867 FireHouse – Hold Your Fire	$18.95
00694894 Frank Gambale – The Great Explorers	$18.95

00694807 Danny Gatton – 88 Elmira St	$17.95
00694848 Genuine Rockabilly Guitar Hits	$19.95
00660326 Guitar Heroes	$17.95
00694780 Guitar School Classics	$17.95
00694768 Guitar School Greatest Hits	$17.95
00694854 Buddy Guy – Damn Right, I've Got The Blues	$18.95
00660325 The Harder Edge	$17.95
00694798 George Harrison Anthology	$19.95
00692930 Jimi Hendrix – Are You Experienced?	$19.95
00692931 Jimi Hendrix – Axis: Bold As Love	$19.95
00660192 The Jimi Hendrix Concerts	$24.95
00692932 Jimi Hendrix – Electric Ladyland	$24.95
00660099 Jimi Hendrix – Radio One	$24.95
00660024 Jimi Hendrix – Variations On A Theme: Red House	$18.95
00660029 Buddy Holly	$18.95
00660200 John Lee Hooker – The Healer	$18.95
00660169 John Lee Hooker – A Blues Legend	$17.95
00694850 Iron Maiden – Fear Of The Dark	$19.95
00694761 Iron Maiden – No Prayer For The Dying	$18.95
00693096 Iron Maiden – Power Slave/Somewhere In Time	$19.95
00693095 Iron Maiden	$22.95
00694833 Billy Joel For Guitar	$18.95
00660147 Eric Johnson Guitar Transcriptions	$18.95
00694799 Robert Johnson – At The Crossroads	$19.95
00693186 Judas Priest – Metal Cuts	$18.95
00660226 Judas Priest – Painkiller	$18.95
00693187 Judas Priest – Ram It Down	$18.95
00693185 Judas Priest – Vintage Hits	$18.95
00694764 Kentucky Headhunters – Pickin' On Nashville	$18.95
00694795 Kentucky Headhunters – Electric Barnyard	$18.95
00660050 B. B. King	$18.95
00694903 The Best Of Kiss	$24.95
00660068 Kix – Blow My Fuse	$18.95
00694806 L.A. Guns – Hollywood Vampires	$18.95
00694794 Best Of Los Lobos	$18.95
00660199 The Lynch Mob – Wicked Sensation	$18.95
00693412 Lynyrd Skynyrd	$18.95
00660174 Yngwie Malmsteen – Eclipse	$18.95
00694845 Yngwie Malmsteen – Fire And Ice	$18.95
00694756 Yngwie Malmsteen – Marching Out	$18.95
00694755 Yngwie Malmsteen's Rising Force	$18.95
00660001 Yngwie Malmsteen Rising Force – Odyssey	$18.95
00694757 Yngwie Malmsteen – Trilogy	$18.95
00692880 Metal Madness	$17.95
00694792 Metal Church – The Human Factor	$18.95
00660229 Monster Metal Ballads	$19.95
00694868 Gary Moore – After Hours	$18.95
00694849 Gary Moore – The Early Years	$18.95
00694802 Gary Moore – Still Got The Blues	$18.95
00694872 Vinnie Moore – Meltdown	$18.95
00694895 Nirvana – Bleach	$18.95
00694913 Nirvana – In Utero	$18.95
00694883 Nirvana – Nevermind	$18.95
00694847 Best Of Ozzy Osbourne	$22.95
00694830 Ozzy Osbourne – No More Tears	$18.95

00694855 Pearl Jam – Ten	$18.95
00693800 Pink Floyd – Early Classics	$18.95
00660188 Poison – Flesh & Blood	$18.95
00693865 Poison – Look What The Cat Dragged In	$18.95
00693864 The Best Of Police	$18.95
00692535 Elvis Presley	$18.95
00693910 Ratt – Invasion of Your Privacy	$18.95
00693911 Ratt – Out Of The Cellar	$18.95
00694892 Guitar Style Of Jerry Reed	$18.95
00694899 REM – Automatic For The People	$18.95
00694898 REM – Out Of Time	$18.95
00660060 Robbie Robertson	$18.95
00694760 Rock Classics	$17.95
00693474 Rock Superstars	$17.95
00694851 Rock: The 50s Volume 1 – Book/Cassette Pack	$19.95
00694902 Rock: The 60s Volume 1 – Book/Cassette Pack	$24.95
00694897 Roots Of Country Guitar	$19.95
00694836 Richie Sambora – Stranger In This Town	$18.95
00694805 Scorpions – Crazy World	$18.95
00694870 Seattle Scene	$18.95
00694885 Spin Doctors – Pocket Full Of Kryptonite	$18.95
00694796 Steelheart	$18.95
00694180 Stryper – In God We Trust	$18.95
00694824 Best Of James Taylor	$14.95
00694846 Testament – The Ritual	$18.95
00694765 Testament – Souls Of Black	$18.95
00694887 Thin Lizzy – The Best Of Thin Lizzy	$18.95
00694410 The Best of U2	$18.95
00694411 U2 – The Joshua Tree	$18.95
00694893 Unplugged – Rock Guitar's Greatest Acoustic Hits	$18.95
00660137 Steve Vai – Passion & Warfare	$24.95
00694904 Vai – Sex and Religion	$19.95
00694879 Stevie Ray Vaughan – In The Beginning	$18.95
00660136 Stevie Ray Vaughan – In Step	$18.95
00660058 Stevie Ray Vaughan – Lightnin' Blues 1983 – 1987	$22.95
00694835 Stevie Ray Vaughan – The Sky Is Crying	$18.95
00694776 Vaughan Brothers – Family Style	$18.95
00660196 Vixen – Rev It Up	$18.95
00694781 Warrant – Cherry Pie	$18.95
00694787 Warrant – Dirty Rotten Filthy Stinking Rich	$18.95
00694866 Warrant – Dog Eat Dog	$18.95
00694789 The Muddy Waters Guitar Collection	$19.95
00694888 Windham Hill Guitar Sampler	$16.95
00694786 Winger	$18.95
00694782 Winger – In The Heart Of The Young	$18.95
00694900 Winger – Pull	$18.95

Prices and availability subject to change without notice.
Some products may not be available outside the U.S.A.

FOR MORE INFORMATION, SEE YOUR LOCAL MUSIC DEALER, OR WRITE TO:

HAL•LEONARD CORPORATION
7777 W. BLUEMOUND RD. P.O. BOX 13819 MILWAUKEE, WI 53213

0294